# Life After Adoption:
## My Unhindered Journey

By
Carolyn Ricks

Published By: TamikaINK

Library of Congress Cataloging-in-Publication Data has been applied for
ISBN: 979-8-8691-7630-1
PRINTED IN THE UNITED STATES OF AMERICA

I dedicate this book to the one who believed in me when no one else did. The woman whose heart I didn't grow under, but I grew *in it*, my mother, the late Nellie Mae King. The one who invested in me, loved me, cared for me, and introduced me to Jesus. I am who I am today because of her and my father, the late Bobbie Lee King. I'll forever make you proud and carry out your legacy.

To my husband, Apostle Jullian Ricks, where would I be had you not found me? I don't even want to think about it. God, you did that! You are absolutely amazing to me and our children: Armonie, Amayah, Amari, Brian, and Julliona! You are selfless, honest, loving, kind, and caring, but most of all, God-fearing, and I'm forever grateful. Thank you for knowing my flaws and loving me unconditionally. I have no regrets in saying I do. It's forever me and you my love.

Lastly, I dedicate this book to my children. Armonie, Amayah, Amari, Brian, and Julliona. Thank you for being patient with me and loving me through the good, bad,  and ugly. It is because of y'all that I pushed, worked so hard, and didn't give up. None of y'all are my mistakes; each one of you is my blessing.

# Table of Contents

## CHAPTER 1

# The Beginning

I was born on March 20, 1980, as Carolyn V. Taylor and was in the foster care system by the time I turned 18 months. I was featured along with my brother on Wavy TV10's "Wednesday's Child," where the news channel featured children in foster care waiting to be adopted. It wasn't hard for my adopted parents, Bobbie Lee King and Nellie Mae King, to adopt us because they were already in the system as foster parents. My adoptive parents told me that they told the agency after seeing me they would adopt me only on one condition, and that was if they could adopt both my biological brother and me to avoid getting us split up.

My biological brother Michael, who is exactly one year older than me, was in the hospital while the adoption was taking place, recovering from burns that had happened to him while in foster care. We will never know exactly what happened to him. The story that was told was that he ran into a tub full of hot water. If that did happen, nothing was at the bottom of his feet. There were burns on his lower back down to his thighs as if someone had dipped him in hot boiling water.

Imagine going into a foster care home wanting to be loved and cared for, but it turns into torment. The foster parents who had us during that time didn't get charged for what they did to my brother. He was hospitalized for months, and they were right there at the hospital. My parents told me that they were asked numerous times if they were sure that they wanted to adopt us both because my brother would need extra care during and after he recovered. Their response never changed. They wanted us both.

After the adoption, my name changed to Carolyn V. King. I grew up with my biological brother and five other siblings in the household; we were called the "King" family. It was a loving but also strict home. I was taught manners and how to respect others, especially adults. They showered us with love, and that's where I learned and developed a relationship with God. My parents kept us in church. It wasn't an option.

We attended Hill Street COGIC under the leadership of then Elder James. J. Johnson, and later, he became the Superintendent of the Suffolk District COGIC. That was my foundation and my upbringing. It was the first church that I ever attended from the time I was adopted at 18 months until around the age of 20. Elder James J. Johnson, now Bishop James J. Johnson, taught us the word of God. There wasn't any playing in church. And if another parent had to discipline us, that was just that, and then we got it again. We sat there and we listened. My mother only had to look at us once, and we knew to straighten up.

I learned to reverence God's house. And to honor and respect it. There was no talking, chewing gum, or even falling asleep. I watched my parents serve there without complaint, and they gave without hesitation. I learned about tithes and offerings there; my father was the chairman deacon. I will say that's where I received so much of my teachings from and those teachings I implement even up to this day. It was there where his daughter, Missionary Sherry Scott, now Evangelist, taught me how to play the tambourine and not to be afraid to sing or talk in front of people. When asked, we just did. Little did I know it was only a training ground for me. I would sing around the altar around the age of 9 years old the hymn "I need thee every hour," and then we prayed.

Growing up, not only did we wear skirts to church and stockings, but my siblings and I only wore skirts to school every day. But I can honestly say my parents had us dressed. We were always clean, and we were always dressed.

By the time I turned 10, I was getting into fights in school. I had a quick temper and would fight quickly. Whenever I got in trouble at school, I would get in trouble at home. Growing up, I didn't get many whoppings but got my share.

At 12 years old, my parents sat my brother Michael and me down and told us that we were adopted, but the two of us were real brothers and sisters. My parents did not have much education, but they knew how to call on the name of the Lord, and my father was a hard worker. Still, to this day, I remember them using the word "real." I honestly didn't know what to feel at that moment when they told me those words, but I knew I wasn't mad or sad. They showed me so much love and treated my brother and me, as well as my other siblings like we were their own.

All I remember saying when she told me was, "Okay."

My mom said she didn't know anything about my real side, but she wouldn't stop us if we wanted to look for them when we got older. My mom was my everything. I knew deep down inside if I did meet my biological mom, I wondered how that would have made my mom feel. So I told her, "No, I won't go looking for her."

All I knew was that she was my mom, and that wouldn't ever change. She was the only mother I knew, and I never wanted to hurt her or make her feel any type of way. She wasn't even built to dislike anyone, but I wanted to protect her and her feelings. I never wanted to disappoint her. I always wanted her to be so proud of me and that her decision to adopt me was one of the best decisions she could have made. I wanted her to feel my love for her.

## CHAPTER 2
# *I'll Never Forget That Day*

By the time I turned 13, I was in eighth grade, which was high school for me. It was there where I acted out. It was there where the feelings of resentment, rejection, and abandonment came over me. It was there where I looked for love in all the wrong places. How could I have all the love in the world shown by parents who spoiled me but still desired more? Could it have been from the parents who never accepted me?

My parents allowed me to be in the marching band, where I was a majorette. I wanted to stay back for the dances and parties, but my parents would not allow me. They would pick me up in their station wagon. I would be so upset because I wanted to stay back and have fun, too. That's when the sneaking out of school came into play. At 13, I got involved with an older guy in high school who was a drummer in the band. I didn't know what I was doing or what I got myself into, but that didn't last long.

At 15, I was involved with another older guy, or, should I say, a grown man, because legally, he was 18. I would skip school and go be with him. I developed feelings for this man and was willing to skip school to be with him. I would even sneak him into my room at my house when my parents weren't home. Until the day came that I didn't see coming. I had skipped school, and we went to a trailer at a trailer park called Red Oakes. I will never forget this day.

I told him my period hadn't come on, and he asked, "Do you know what this could mean? You could be pregnant."

I wasn't thinking about anything like that. So he left me there and went to the store to buy me a pregnancy test, and when he came back, I took it. And there I was, pregnant at the age of fifteen. I didn't know what to do. How could I tell my parents such a thing? Not only did I not know what to do, but I didn't know who to tell. So I didn't. And he talked me into getting an abortion.

I had no clue of what I was doing or the effect this would have on me years later. All I knew was that I didn't want my parents, let alone anyone, to find out. I didn't even know the stipulations of being adopted. What would happen to me? And I didn't want my mom to have to go through anything all because of me. Most importantly, the embarrassment.

There were so many things that went through my head. So I told him that I would do it, and he took me to this abortion clinic in Newport News, VA, and handed me the money, and I went in. I don't know what I signed I just signed some papers, gave the lady the cash he gave me, and I did it. I left out crying and hurt, and he and his grandmother picked me up. *I'll never forget that day.*

## CHAPTER 3

# Broken and Scarred – The Grind Never Stopped

After the abortion, that's when feelings of guilt came over me. I did ask God to forgive me, but the guilt still remained. Days later, I received a phone call from the same man whose child I had just aborted girlfriend. She asked me what my prescription papers were doing in his pocket. I was speechless, and I just hung up the phone. I was a fool to think that I was the only one he was dealing with, and on top of that, I was still trying to heal from what had just happened. That was a different kind of hurt. I even became angry. I stopped dealing with him for a while after that, and I kept this in. This is the first time

I have released it publicly. My mom ended up finding out about this after I was grown. And she told me that she wished I had told her. Had I known that would have been her response, I wished I had told her too. I became somewhat promiscuous after that.

By the time I turned 18, I was pregnant again. So, in my 12th grade year, I walked around pregnant. I got involved with another older man who was 25. I told my parents this time, got through my 12th grade school year with flying colors, and graduated right on time. I never had a problem with getting my work done. I had plans to go into the military immediately after high school, but that changed.

I had my firstborn, Armonie Shadae' King. She was such a beautiful baby. She was dark-skinned with beautiful skin and beautiful curly hair. I worked and had my own apartment and my own car at eighteen. I wasn't in love with her father I was just with him. But I loved our child together. It was having her that I told myself I would never abandon any of my kids.

At age 20, I began working at a packing plant called Smithfield Packing. I met a guy who was talking Jesus and nice-looking to me at the same time who pursued me. I just knew my mom would love him, especially proclaiming to be saved. He talked about marriage and how he would treat me like a Queen. I jumped in it way too soon. I got into a relationship that led to a marriage that lasted about six months.

This man beat me so much. He would even stick guns inside of my mouth. Those few months with him felt like years of torture. He would do crazy things like jump out of the car while I was driving or say he would do something to himself. I remember a worker named Cynthia Smith, who was assigned to me during this time. I guess you could call her a case worker. She came into my life at the right time. She was with an agency called "Healthy Families," and she helped that marriage get annulled. It was like we never got married. Only to find myself pregnant with his child.

I contemplated getting an abortion. I never wanted to see that man again. But I couldn't bring myself to do it again. Every year that passed, I would say I would have such a sweet ___year old. I thought about whether it was a boy or a girl. I just couldn't. So I had her, Amayah Shamae' Hughes, and I am so glad I did.

While I was pregnant, I became friends with a guy who was so nice to me and treated me with so much respect and loved my oldest and the one I was pregnant with before she was even born. I could not believe how this man was treating me, knowing this was not his child, and here I am with this big stomach and a child. That's when the feeling of insecurities came in. Anything that I needed, he gave me. He was so cool. When I had Amayah, he gave her the nickname "Boosie," which took after his nickname "BooBoo."

He made sure he provided everything and anything that they needed. That friendship led to a relationship, a long one at that. My parents loved him. They watched how he cared for us. I stayed in that relationship on and off for about five years. We had a child and lived together, and he proposed to me, but we didn't get married. He started cheating, and I started doing my own thing. I dealt with rejection and abandonment for so long that I was prepared for whomever to walk out of my life, or I would try to walk out of theirs before they did. He continued cheating and married my cousin. We were cousins up until she started messing with him, then it was, "Well, we're not blood cousins."

Some of my family agreed to that, and I was shocked! The betrayal. I grew up around this girl as family. She saw how he treated me, and she jumped on it. I can't front, I was hurt, but I moved on.

I felt like the outcast in my family a lot from my siblings with whom I was raised. It was like I was always talked about, and on top of that, one sister in particular sided with my cousin who married my daughter's father, and they became so tight. But I sucked it up. Even if I was hurt, I tried not to show it.

Now, here I am, a single mother with three kids and three baby daddies...Broken and scarred, I was, but I never let anything or anyone stop my grind. I was a hard worker, and still am to this day. I got my work ethic from both my parents.

I was still at Smithfield Packing plant, but by age 23, I got promoted and got an office job in the customer service department. I had favor back then and didn't even realize it. I knew I didn't belong on that assembly line and wanted more for myself. There was so much drama on the inside of the plant. Truthfully, I did some things wrong in there that I should not have done and am not proud of. But I knew that promotion came from God, and I worked hard and earned that position. There, I fell in love with the office setting and learned as much as possible in a professional setting. I loved the professional atmosphere. There was less drama in the office. I stayed in that position for about two years.

## CHAPTER 4

# The Visitation

Now to the year of 2005. I'm 25 years old now. This is the year when I feel like my life changed drastically. I was in church, but I wasn't all the way in. I had one foot in and one foot out. Although I had been in church all my life, I still wanted to go out to clubs and parties. I had two close friends, but Shanna Glover was my girl. We had been friends since we were like 13. My mom would pick her up in the station wagon while en route to church, and she would go with us. We just banged, and 30 years later, we still do. She respects who I am today. She never switched up on me, nor has she ever changed. She's a real one.

Shanna called me Kesh, short for Keisha, from the movie "Belly." I had the looks, but I had a streak in me that played no games and didn't care. I never was afraid to fight. I learned later that came from my biological side. I never drank, and I never smoked a day in my life, but I was the one who would put on the real tight and short clothes to go out, and on the flip side, I would still go to church.

I started working at a Collection Agency in Newport News, Va. They offered me more money and opportunities for a bonus so I couldn't refuse that offer. I became so good at collecting that I started getting bonuses of a couple thousand dollars extra each month. For a 25-year-old who had responsibilities, that was right on time. You couldn't tell me nothing!

My parents helped me purchase my first home. It was a mobile home, but I owned it, and

28

it was really nice. At this time, I began attending a church named Cathedral of Life UHCOL (United Holiness Churches of Life) along with my parents under the leadership of Bishop William Blackwell Sr. They were friends of my parents. They loved my parents, and my parents loved them. It was a Holiness church, and I found myself at the altar every Sunday. It seemed like I was trying hard to keep my flesh under control. But I kept on attending, knowing the things I was doing weren't right. But they never judged me.

I served there, and it was there where I first preached; later on, it was there where I witnessed deliverance take place. I mean, I witnessed spirits talk back. It was there where I also served. I would put services on, and I sang. It was there where not only my leader and Bishop at the time told me I would preach, but also my mother told me I would preach and that there was a major call on my life. I didn't want to accept it at the time. I knew what I was doing was contrary to the word of God.

My mother would tell me, "Carolyn, it's better not to make a promise to God than to make one and break it." She literally put the fear of God in me. She would tell all of us that God will soon return. But deep down, I wasn't ready. I also knew if I gave God a real "yes," I would be true to the call.

So, I stayed single and continued doing what I wanted to do. I started dealing with someone at the job at the collection agency I was working at who had a high-end position there. We acted as if we weren't dealing with each other and always kept it professional. It was just something to do whenever I wanted — no strings attached.

I worked, cared for my girls, went out when I wanted, and still attended church. I had to pass by my parent's home to get to my house, so it was nothing for me to stop by almost every day. The kids were practically over there all the time. I never wanted to neglect them or make them feel unwanted, but my parents loved them and wanted them there as much as they wanted to be there. I never wanted them to experience anything I went through, so I was always there for them, giving them everything they wanted. They always had the best, and I took really good care of them.

Still, in 2005, I got what I believed was my wake-up call. The night I almost lost my life. Now, remember, I never drank or smoked. But on this particular night, while leaving a club at about 1:00 am, I was driving home, and I thought to myself that I was going to stay at my parent's house because the hour was late and since I had to pass by there to get home, I told myself I would just stay there and just go to church from there in the morning. I remember being almost to their house; all I could remember was a huge deer jumping out in front of me. I swerved to avoid hitting the deer and went over to the other side of the highway. My car kept flipping and flipping and flipping (I found out later that my car flipped five times), and I got thrown out.

I am standing outside my car, and I turn around only to see the car upside down. Here, I am in the middle of a very dark field with roads with no street lights. I then looked down at my body, and I saw that my body was still intact. I remember crying out to God, saying, "Lord, I thank you," and then I blacked out.

The accident was literally about seven miles from my parent's house. All I remember next was standing on my parents' porch and my mom opening the door. I asked her how I got there, and she told me she heard the doorbell ring (Still, to this day, I still don't know how I got there, and no one ever came forward). I went inside, and she could see blood over my legs. I told her I was in an accident and that I was tasting blood. She told me that wasn't a good sign, so she called the ambulance.

When the ambulance got there and checked my vitals, they could not find a pulse, so they called for Nightingale. I remember on Nightingale, they asked me questions and talked, but I couldn't answer. What I was doing was praying inwardly, and I asked the Lord. "Lord, if you bring me through this, I'll serve you for the rest of my life."

The next thing I remember was being in what looked to be a surgery room. My eyes were open by this time, and the doctor asked me what had happened. I told him I swerved off the road to avoid hitting a deer. He told me that the next time, I needed to hit the deer because I could have lost my life avoiding hitting deer. I knew it was God trying to get my attention. But I just nodded.

They first thought I needed a blood transfusion because I had internal bleeding, but that changed. I had prayer warriors on post praying and interceding for me. My parents and my Bishop were praying and believing God for a miracle. So I wasn't shocked that my report changed and there was no need for a blood transfusion. I walked out of that hospital three days later with only a broken wrist and deep scars from the glass on my thigh. That's what I get from barely having clothes on.

After that happened and the vow that I made to God, I was on fire for him. I threw all of my rap and R&B CDs away. I stopped clubbing, and I stopped messing around. The thought of sin vexed me. I was witnessing and telling others about Christ and how he saved me. I was telling my testimony everywhere. I was what they call "super saved." I was reading my Word all the time. I was all in. I was having dreams, and I had a visitation. I have always been a dreamer. My dreams would be so strong they would scare me by how quickly they came to pass.

The visitation I had was with an Angel. I was at my mother's house in a back room sleeping. I was awakened by what felt like a strong wind, to the point that it felt like my chest was out of my body. It was very strong. I laid my head back down and heard a voice say to me, "Fear not, for I am always with you."

I moved the cover back and saw the body, but I didn't look up at the face. The body was all white, wrapped in white linen but extremely white, and what surrounded the body in a circular motion was glistening. The glistening looked like a firecracker when it hit the air, but it was beautiful and radiant colors. I can't describe the glistening color, but it was so beautiful. I still don't know why I didn't look all the way up at the face, but with the covers halfway over my face, I started smiling so hard. And then that same wind that came in that woke me up I felt again when the Angel left. I was so happy, shocked, and honored that this happened to me.

The next morning, I told my mom what happened, and she was so happy that I experienced that. She was always so happy with what made me happy and concerned with what concerned me. But she was a woman of Faith. She taught me everything spiritually and naturally. I wish I had watched her cook more. She knew how to save money, and she taught me how, too. Did I always listen to everything? No. She instilled in us early the importance of having great credit. My mom had excellent credit; she could cook meals, she kept all of us clean and nice, and we had chores. They had a house built from the ground up, property and land, and they drove nice cars. She taught us early that "You may not have money in your pocket, but you will still eat if you have great credit."

## CHAPTER 5

### *On Fire For God*

A couple of years passed by, and it's now 2007, and yes, I'm still on fire for God. I met my biological sisters thanks to my mom allowing them to visit us as a teenager. But now it was time that I met my biological mother, Debra Pitt. I was 27 years old with three beautiful girls and on my own. I visited my biological sister Kindala's "Kin" house to meet her. '

When I first saw her, I was speechless. I looked exactly like this woman. And she said to me those exact words that I looked just like her. She was open to any questions, but I just couldn't open myself up to ask her any. I still can't put into words that day. My mother, who raised me, instilled in me love, and in church, I learned about forgiveness. If God could forgive me after everything I did, I knew I could forgive anyone, even without an apology.

I continued being on fire for God. I found myself in church and witnessing to people every chance I got. There was a revival taking place in Smithfield, and the host church had brought in a well-known young prophet from out of state. News traveled fast in that small town of Smithfield. I mean, everybody knows everybody. So, I went to hear him along with Bishop Blackwell Sr.'s daughter, Keisha Blackwell-Green, who I call my sis. The service was good. I had already been exposed to the prophetic, but this was on another level for me. He called names, even mine, and on that night, he spoke a word into my life that I knew could only come from God.

I remember him laying hands on me, and I hit the floor. The power of God was so strong. I continued to attend that revival, and my mom even went with me one night. I also continued following his ministry, and one night, he broke down (Biblically) the importance of getting baptized in Jesus' name, so I got baptized again, but this time in Jesus' name (Acts 2:38 KJV). My co-worker at the time told me her church baptized every Sunday in Jesus' name, and I went there to the Messiah Center located in Hampton, Va.

After I got baptized in Jesus' name, I was filled with the Holy Spirit with the evidence of tongues. I literally went to another place in God, and I loved that feeling. I continued following the ministry of that prophet while still attending my church, of course. But one night after he was in revival at a church in Suffolk, VA, he came up to me and told me to wait for him, and I did. He gave me his number, and I gave him mine. We spoke over the phone, just a casual conversation at first. I was definitely intrigued with the anointing that was on his life. It would be out of the blue, and he would tell me things that I went through verbatim and even names of people that were so shocking.

We continued talking. But then things shifted. He would come into town and would tell me where he was staying, and I'd go, and that's what started me back to doing those things that I used to do. I was reverting back to my old ways. I got myself into a trap. I felt so bad afterward because now I have the Holy Ghost and was convicted. But I kept doing it. He gave me a 2-carat diamond ring and so much money even though I had money. But I got sucked into that life all over again.

I would still go to my church, and I knew my behavior changed, but I still tried to tap in spiritually and couldn't. I tried to fake what I was in, knowing my Bishop had seen right through me. Until one night, my Bishop had a guest Prophetess come. I'll never forget. She could preach and prophesy. She walked up to me and told me the one I was with was not the one, and the one God has for me will love me for me and love my children.

I got so mad, and I didn't want to receive that at all. And I had the ring on my finger, thinking I was something. Everyone at the service knew I was bothered by what she said. You could see it on my face. If only I had heeded the warning. Instead, I continued messing with him. He would come into town, and I would go to his hotel after he preached. Back then, I could pick up on things, especially body language, and

I knew I wasn't the only one he was dealing with. Other girls would sit in the same service and wait to see him afterward.

I started hearing that he had other women in other states, but I continued messing with him. I was back in sin all over again. I started back talking to the one I was dealing with at the job on and off periodically. I felt myself spiritually shifting. I was going backward. And then here it goes: I found out that I was pregnant.

I was devastated. I thought about taking the easy way out and not going through with the pregnancy. I thought about what the church world would say and potentially losing my witness. I had ones to tell me I should term it, and of course, the father didn't want me to go through with the pregnancy. Little did they know that was something I had already done before and that guilt and pain was on another level. Instead, I kept the baby and went through with the pregnancy.

I continued on going to church. I wasn't as active, but they didn't make me feel like an outcast either. I continued putting services together, one being youth revivals. I would ask Elder Pierre to come and preach, and he would bring a musician named Jullian "Paco" Ricks. I didn't know it then, but Jullian was watching me this entire time. After service during the youth revival, mind you; I'm showing. To me, I felt like I was as big as a house. Jullian approached me just to speak, noticed the 2-carat ring on my finger, and said, "That's a nice ring." I thanked him for that compliment.

I found out that I was having a boy, and after having three girls, I was happy about that. However, there were many things that went through my head, and it was then that I was diagnosed with hypertension and put on high-blood pressure pills. I gave birth to a healthy baby boy on September 26, 2008. I was numb to pain, so I just dealt with it as it came.

On the road to celebrate my son's first birthday, my father passed. It was on September 12, 2009. It was all of a sudden. Outside of my father being a hard worker, he loved the outdoors. He would work outside in our yard a lot. We had a garden, and I would even go out into the garden with him. We had to go out to the clothesline to hang clothes out. There was no washing clothes in the washing machine.

I remember him coming into the house, and there was a small lump on his back. I even felt it with my own hands, and we all told him we didn't think it was serious, but he ended up getting it checked out, and it was cancer, and it was already at Stage 4. We were told it was too late, and it started spreading. There were no signs of him having anything as such. And we believed God for a miracle. We kept praying and praying. But I did see this coming. I dreamed that the immediate family was at a repass and balloons went up in the air. I confirmed with my dream interpreter what the dream was about, so I knew it, but I didn't want to accept it, and I believed God would heal him.

His passing took a toll on all of us, especially my mom, who was married to my father for 49 years. He praised God until his last breath. He was in the house when he passed, and I sang, "I am Free, praise the Lord, I am free." My mom told him how much of a great husband and father he was, and we watched him take his last breath. I witnessed my mother's strength displayed on another level. I even shouted at his homegoing.

My mom still came to my son's first birthday party. It was around that time that I cut my hair. I wanted a different look, but I know now I was dealing with depression and disappointment.

## CHAPTER 6

*Nothing Else Mattered*

I continued taking care of my children and letting them go to my mom's house to spend time with her. She loved all children, but she loved herself her grandchildren. I had it good; not only did she keep them for me, but help raise them and helped me as a parent. There was no illness for which she did not have an old remedy that did not work.

My ex and I tried to come to an agreement financially as well as a mutual understanding as it relates to my son, and he called himself bringing in his friend, another well-known pastor. This pastor flew in from another state. He came to help us reach this mutual agreement only to try and holla at me. I was so hurt about everything that had happened and me being shunned that before I knew it, we had messed around. He came in a few other times to preach, and we met up a couple of more times after that. I was in my feelings as well as grieving the loss of my father. But I took full ownership of my actions; I knew what I was doing.

I did date a preacher for a short period of time who was actually a very nice man. I actually thought we would get married. We didn't attend the same church growing up, but we were part of the same fellowship. He chose to be with someone else whom he ended up marrying. God knows all.

There came a time when I was over doing the things that I was doing. I needed healing and deliverance. I always felt convicted of going to services knowing what I was doing. I sang on the praise team and praised, knowing my actions were wrong. I decided to get the deliverance that I needed. I repented and cried out to the Lord to help and deliver me! I knew that God was the only one that could do this. My mother would tell me all the time that I didn't want to die in my sin.

Something came over me. I heard the Lord say to me that if I do it His way, He will bless me. And so I got the deliverance and healing that I needed and got back on track. I closed my legs, got in my word, got closer to God, and didn't look back. I was determined not to go backward again. I had girls and a son watching me. I would not let anything stop me from getting all the blessings that God had in store for me. I had been through so much. I went broken before the Lord so he could mend my heart and mend my broken pieces.

It's 2011, and I am now 31 years old and still on track. Still going after God like never before. I started attending another church in Smithfield under Pastor Kerry White. I was a faithful member and giver. I never struggled with money or giving. I watched my mom for years give and I watched how she handled her business. The kids are now 13, 11, 7, and 3. I took them to church. It wasn't an option. I wanted them raised in church like I was; that was my foundation and upbringing. I knew how to act in church. My siblings and I paid attention, and if it looked like we were playing or talking, my mom would give us an eye, and that got us together.

At this church, I was active. I love to sing, and I would sing on the praise team. I worked, and I kept myself busy at church. I still worked for the same collection agency. By this time, I had been promoted to account manager and had a team that worked only on weekends under me while I still collected during the week. One day at work, the AVP at the time, Zoe, asked me to go with her to the store to get some sandwich meat. She was expecting at the time, so this was a craving for her. I went across the street to the Food Lion along with her. Little did I know at the time that it was God at work.

As soon as I got out of the car, I saw Jullian. Back then, his nickname was "Paco," and that's what I called him. Now, remember he was the same one who played the keyboard for the guest preacher for the revivals I put on while attending Cathedral of Life.

He was like, "Hey Carolyn," and I was like, "Hey," and he asked how I had been. We exchanged numbers, but it was more so as friends. At least, that's how I was looking at it only. I was definitely not looking for a relationship at the time. I was actually living right and focused.

I continued on with my day, but that night, I started getting a bunch of notifications on Facebook of all of my pictures being liked by him. I never minded it, but that night, he called me. I had never been on the phone with a man that was so respectful. He was so nice, and he wanted to get to know me. I mean, we talked for hours. He would invite me to different programs he had at his church, but it seemed like I always had something going on. Until, finally, he invited me to a service, and I was able to attend.

I called my close friend Shauniqua Bland to come with me. Shauniqua knew of him and told me I should talk to him, but I didn't want to. She was the kind of friend who always kept it real, and we would talk for hours about the things of God. We always encouraged one another and spoke into each other's lives. One of us would prophesy, and then the other would. We bumped heads at times, too, but that's because we both stood on what we believed. We both had strong personalities. So she was down for attending that service with me.

We went, and we had such a wonderful time. I enjoyed the speaker, but what stood out to me was how Jullian worshipped. It was genuine, and it was real. But even after seeing that, I was so scared. I saw the preachers who were preaching and then trying to get me to their room. I wasn't going back there. But I didn't want to have a wall up either just by how he carried himself. He was different. We spoke that night, and I thanked him for inviting me. We continued talking, and after a couple of months, we went on our first date to Five Guys.

We had such a great conversation, but what stood out to me was that he wanted to know about each one of my children. He remembered their names after I told him only one time. He was into our conversation. When it was time to leave, he walked me to my car. I couldn't believe that he was such the perfect gentleman. This man wasn't trying to take me to a hotel or trying to get to my house. I was shocked. I couldn't believe it. We continued dating and getting to know each other. I remember him telling me, "I'm going to go to God, and if He tells me that you are my wife, I'm going to marry you."

Who me? I had so many insecurities. I was like, who would marry me with four children with different fathers? I knew I could "mess" with anybody, but who would actually wife me? I prayed, and I asked God to heal and free me from lust, pain from the past, disappointments, rejection, abandonment, and the feeling of loneliness, and He did just that. But now I needed God to heal my insecurities. I would read scriptures like Psalms 139:14 KJV *I will praise thee; for I am fearfully and wonderfully made: marvelous are thy works; and that my soul knoweth right well.*

After a couple of months, I then started developing feelings for a man that I didn't even have sex with, and I couldn't believe it. I asked God to show me a clear sign that I couldn't miss it if he was the one. I asked God to allow the man he had for me to love me, my children, and one who would respect the girls. So, while he was praying to God for a release on asking me to be his wife, I asked God for a sign if he was my husband. And so I had a dream, and in this dream, a very elderly man, Jullian, and I were in what looked to be a rocket. We all had on all white, and all of a sudden, while the elderly man who was in charge touched the wheel of the rocket, we shot off into space really fast. I can't explain how fast we were going, but it was extremely fast, and we were so happy. I reached out to my friend, whom I call my sis, who has the gift to interpret dreams, Keisha Blackwell-Green, and she told me that the man in the dream would pave the way for us to where we were going.

Around three months into the relationship, he picked me up because he wanted me to meet his grandfather. I had already fallen in love with his mom. She was the absolute sweetest to me and the kids. So, here we were at his grandfather's house. He told me that his grandfather helped raise him, that he was the man he looked up to, that he was still preaching and teaching the word even at 95 years old, and that he was sharp spiritually. He told me that he was blind in one eye and partially blind in the other, but you would feel the power of God as soon as he opened his mouth.

I was looking forward to meeting him. I don't know if it was because my parents were older when they adopted me or what, but I always loved being around older people. I still do. We went into his grandfather's house, and as soon as I laid my eyes on him, I was speechless. He was the same exact man who was in the rocket with us in my dream. I whispered to Jullian that he was the same man in my dream and I couldn't believe it.

Jullian said to him, "Daddie (what they affectionately called him), this is Carolyn."

His grandfather replied, "Oh yes, Carolyn Virginia."

I wanted to run right out the door because no one knew my middle name I didn't tell anyone because I didn't like it. I asked Jullian, "How in the world did he know that?"

I responded, "Yes, sir, I am so happy to meet you!"

Jullian was so happy he got his approval because he valued his grandfather's words.

Everyone wasn't happy for us. There were many people, more so church folk, who felt he should be with someone who didn't have any children. Here I am, 31 years old with four kids, and him being 27 years old with no children. They didn't know just how established I was. I'm talking about how I was already a homeowner who had great credit, a great-paying job, and much money in the bank. To them, I was just a girl with a bunch of kids. Not so. I was a strong, independent, grown woman with children who were well taken care of. On top of that, believe it or not, I knew there was a major call on my life, so I knew I was what he needed spiritually and naturally.

We talked about *everything*. The more he made me feel special, and the more I felt protected by him, the more I shared with him. When I told him about my past, I was so ashamed and embarrassed, but he made me feel like I was still a queen, like I was somebody. And I made him feel like the King he was. I watched him have no bank account and go to the store to cash his checks after playing for hours; I watched his car get repossessed, and I watched him have no medical or dental insurance. I watched him struggle. And so I asked him if he wanted more for himself. I asked him where he wanted his credit score to be and that I would help him get there. I told him it would take discipline, but if he did it my way, he would have great credit, a home, and multiple bank accounts. As we continued dating, I saw so much in him beyond him just playing the keyboard. I witnessed a prophetic call on his life.

There were people who wanted him with other women who thought they were a better fit than me, so we broke up in October. He actually told me he needed some time to think, fast, and pray. I told him, "Okay," and even though I knew what God showed me in the dream, which was my sign, I was okay with it. During that week, he fell short and needed something to eat. He asked if I could order some food for him, and I told him, "No, I cannot (even though I could have). But since you need time to pray, figure out how you gonna eat." (Lol)

We actually broke up for about one week, and because he told me he needed time to think and pray, I knew it was more. See, some women don't want you, but they don't want anybody else to have you. But Lord knows I wanted him to be whole before marriage, and I also wanted to be whole.

My girl Shauniqua ended up talking to us both, and she told him I was his wife, but he told her he was praying. A week later, he pulled up at my mother's house with a card and my favorite chocolate and told me he never wanted to let me go and that I was the one. I knew it was real, and he was being honest. Of course, I took him back, and six months into our relationship, he proposed to me on December 21, 2011. He was supposed to propose to me on Christmas Day, but he was so excited that he couldn't wait those four days. He picked up the ring from the jewelry store, and when he got back in the car, he proposed, and without hesitation, I said, "Yes."

I knew it was God ordained. He didn't want to wait long, and honestly, neither did I. He knew I was his Ruth, and I knew he was my Boaz. My flesh started to cut up, so we both agreed to get married six months later. I wanted a nice wedding. I wanted a church wedding with a long aisle to give everyone a chance to look at me good. After all that I had been through in my life, that was my day, and it was my time.

I literally had six months to make my dream a reality, and we needed money. My mother helped us out tremendously, which became the talk of the town I was from. I couldn't believe one of my sisters, whom I was raised with, envied me so much that she started rumors and talked about us so badly. Some of them said the most hurtful things, like how my fiancé was broke and didn't have any money and how my mom paid for everything.

I was raised in such a small town where everybody knew everybody. But the truth of the matter is my mother loved me. She loved all of us as if we were her own biological children. And on top of that, she loved my children, and honestly, some family members were just jealous. I couldn't care less about their opinions. I knew God had blessed me with a good man. I didn't care if he didn't have a lot of money. I knew he loved God and wasn't putting on a front and that he genuinely loved me. I knew it, and God confirmed it.

There was something else I needed to do as I prepared myself for marriage. I knew I had to get rid of those soul ties. I prayed to God, and

I told the Lord that I only wanted eyes and desires for my husband. I didn't want to marry him and be thinking about another man. I watched my parents' marriage, and it was beautiful. I'm sure they had good and bad days, but we never witnessed them being at each other's throats. I watched them both care for each other. I watched them teach us and train us up in the way we should go. I watched them carry us to church. I watched my mom cook meals every day and handle the finances. She had excellent credit, a nice home, and cars, but most importantly, they loved the Lord.

So, back to getting rid of those soul ties. I was serious. So, after we both prayed, we went to a friend of ours named Prophetess Lena, and she prayed over us, and the power of God rested upon us. I remember crying out to God that night and asking him all over again to forgive me for every man that I'd laid with before marriage and to cleanse me from all unrighteousness (1 John 1:9 KJV). When we left there, I felt light as a feather.

We also started marriage counseling with my spiritual father, Bishop Blackwell Sr. The counseling was so good; he was full of wisdom. We talked about finances and that I would be the one who handled them, but for me to always remember, he was still the head of the house. That part wasn't hard because I watched my mom still respect and honor her spouse, even handling the finances.

Even while dating, I never let Jullian feel insecure about his finances or feel bad about not having a lot of money because I knew that would change with the tools I had learned over the years. If we were out and he didn't have the money, I would slip him my card as if he paid. I covered him, and he covered me.

In counseling, we also talked about who would discipline the kids. We decided that I would be the one to administer any spankings if I deemed it necessary, and his form of discipline would be to talk to the children if needed. And that worked for us. Not only for our co-parenting style but also because the children really respected and listened to him. We had good children. Yes, there were attitudes here and there, but we handled it *together* as a unified front.

In marriage counseling, we also had to decide on which church we would attend together, which was difficult because I loved my church, and he loved his and was the minister of music there. I ended up going to his, but not for long. I just didn't feel settled there. Honestly, I just wanted us to start somewhere fresh together where we could grow together, and I felt comfortable there. So we left his church a month before we got married. We both agreed that we would continue counseling with my former Bishop, whom I looked at and still do as my spiritual father throughout our marriage. Wherever we ended up attending as well, we both agreed that he would be the one to marry us.

I was in love with this man that God had blessed me with. After all of the things that I had been through in my life, I couldn't wait to marry him. After six months of dating and six months of planning, we married on June 9, 2012. Our wedding was so beautiful. Our colors were amethyst and grey, with a splash of pink. We had swans made as a backdrop. All of the decorations were stunning.

My mother and both his parents were there and happy. If only my father lived to see the man I know he prayed would find me. He had some of my father's attributes, and I wished he could have met him. I know my father would have loved him and would have been crazy about how well he played the organ, but most importantly, how he loved God and my children. It was just how my father loved my siblings and me, and none of us were actually his.

We didn't have much money after the wedding, so we decided to stay at a hotel in Smithfield, and then we went to King's Dominion, and I was okay with that for a honeymoon. Nothing else mattered.

## CHAPTER 7

*I Believed Him*

Since my mobile home, which was very nice, was paid for, we decided that it made more sense and "cents" for him to move into my place. It was still important to me that I made him feel like the king of the house. We had lot rent to pay, car payments, and other bills here and there. He had a car, but it ended up getting repossessed. He kept those things from me. I don't know why, but I knew I had to help him financially and with budgeting if we would establish anything together.

Because I was so open with him, he knew the car I drove my ex helped me with, and then on top of that, he knew my parents had helped me pay my house off. He wanted us to get things and wanted us to have the best. I told him it wasn't going to happen overnight. He had to be disciplined, and even though he got paid decent on Sundays for playing the organ, he would need another source of income to pay off debt, and then we could establish things together.

At the beginning of our relationship, he gave me the fake bags, and I rocked them. He told me, "One day, imma get you a real Louis Vuitton."

He told me we would purchase a house together, and even though I didn't see it, I believed him. I did assure him that I wasn't impressed with the materialistic things. I had been with men with money, but they didn't treat me worth anything. I was just a jump off to them, so I honestly wasn't into it.

Jullian treated me so well and respected me as if I was the best thing that happened to him. We had fun, and we liked the same things. He never gave me a reason not to trust him. But I didn't want him to ever leave me, and I never wanted to walk away.

But one night, I went through his phone. My mother told me if you go looking for stuff, you'll find it. I was being really noisy. I didn't see any text messages or anything that wasn't supposed to be in there, but I went through old Facebook messages like an idiot. I should not have cared about his past like he didn't care about mine when I told him. But I saw old conversations from about two girls he used to try to holla at, but one of them didn't give him any play, and I have to admit I'm glad they didn't; it was their loss and my gain, lol!

But there was one who he told me they were close friends, and she even became my friend because they were close, but as I read, I was like, "Wait a minute, this sounds more than they were only close friends," and I was heated. I'm like, he didn't tell me this, and even though it's old, I had told him everything. I mean some shameful things, and I was calling her my friend. Even when we broke up, she prayed with me and told him I was the one. I woke him up and asked, "Why didn't you tell me this?"

He was like, "You went through my phone? You don't trust me?"

I was still going off. And then I asked him a question I probably shouldn't have asked since I'd already seen the nature of their past conversations, "Did y'all mess around with each other back then?"

And he answered, "Yes, we did, but we decided that we would only stick to being friends."

I asked, "Why didn't you just tell me? Why did you leave that part out?" He told me because they were *only* friends.

I told him I felt like he should have told me that part, too, even though she never made me feel like there was more. She was actually a genuine, sweet person. I don't know why; I just didn't want him to have ever been with anybody else, lol.

I got over it, but I did ask if there was anything else he thought I should know and to forget the don't ask, don't tell mindset, and he told me no. But I never have to worry about him ever stepping out on his marriage because God blessed him when he allowed him to find me, and I will always honor the vows he made.

He also told me his father left his mom for another woman when he was nine years old and how he remembered his mom, even at nine, hurt so bad and would stay in bed when he left for school, and when he came home, she would still be there with the pillow over her head hurt and he told himself then that when he got married, he would never do that to his wife and I believed him.

## CHAPTER 8

*Enjoy All The Favor You Obtained When You Married Me!*

For us, I feel like our first year of marriage was challenging only in the area of money. I knew he made decent money only playing, but I told him if he worked, that would be extra income, and in order for us to obtain more and get things along with me, he needed another job, and so he did. I was so proud of him. We lived in Windsor, VA, so he went to an assistant living home for a housekeeping position, but when the hiring manager looked at his application and called him, he told him I see you in management. What would be a $7.50 hourly position turned into a management position and salary-paying job. I was so happy, and I knew he had a favor. The word says in Proverbs 18:22 KJV, *"Whoso findeth a wife findeth a good thing, and obtaineth favour of the LORD."*

I would always tell him, "Enjoy all that favor you obtained when you married me."

We continued going to the church we chose to attend as a family. But we still sought marriage counsel from Bishop Blackwell, who married us. We both knew we had major calls on our lives. I definitely was running from it, and so was he.

January 2013, while we were all headed to church in my 2007 Honda Accord, It was extremely foggy and raining. I was driving, and I remember Jullian telling me to be careful, and as soon as I said, "I got it," I lost control of the car, and the car flipped into a deep ditch.

I remember exclaiming, "Oh my God! Everybody say something so I can know everyone is okay!"

We only had the three girls in the back; our son had stayed with my mom. My husband crawled through the sunroof and pulled each one of us out by hand. We all went to the hospital in the ambulance, and we all got discharged the same day. We all made it out alive. The accident mentally messed with one of the girls, and she didn't want to ride with us for a while. It took some time, but she eventually came around.

Months later, still in 2013, my husband told me that God had been dealing with him and speaking to him about ministry. He told me that it was time for him to answer the call on his life. I would witness the prophetic in his life, and I also knew he was living right. I told him I knew it was on him, and he had my full support in ministry. We planned to begin holding evening services a few months later. We still had a home church and intended to serve there as well until God called us completely out.

Now that we were in agreement, there was the matter of telling our pastor. After my husband told him, the Pastor stood up during the next Sunday service and told the congregation, "This will be the Ricks' last Sunday here. They said that God called them to Pastor."

He also told the congregation that he would never stand in our way of what God told us to do, but "Just leave with who you came with, which is only your family."

My husband was hurt because it *wasn't* our last Sunday; the pastor made that decision for us. So, we sought counsel from Bishop Blackwell Sr., who told us to answer the call and that he would be there for us. And he was with us every step of the way.

We prayed, and the Lord gave my husband specific instructions. We started off May 2013 with Friday Night services at 6 PM. Bishop Blackwell allowed us to use his church and we started off with our family and one other family. Then, a few other families started attending. We had *good* church. I watched many people get saved right off the streets, filled with the Holy Ghost (Acts 2:4), and be on fire for God. I knew then that it was a deliverance ministry. I watched my husband prophesy to people, and things came to pass so quickly. And on September 2013, my husband was ordained Elder and affirmed Pastor, and I was licensed as a minister.

## CHAPTER 9

# *We Believed God For A Miracle*

My husband was now the Pastor, and I was the Co-Pastor of the Church of Destiny. I had been in church all my life and was already a hard worker. I knew how to put services and programs together. My husband had sat under his grandfather, Bishop W.J. Sellers, all his life as well. He helped raise him, so church wasn't new to us, but *Pastoring* was. You just better know it's what God called you to do. We both did everything for a while, and then the Lord sent us help. My mom and his mom believed in us, but I had other family who still talked about us so badly. However, we kept doing what the Lord instructed us to do.

So here you have it: we married in 2012, and in 2013, a year later, we started a church. In August 2013, I discovered I was pregnant, and we both were extremely happy. This was his first child; even though I had four, I still wanted him to enjoy his first experience. I told him that it was okay that he was overjoyed and that if he wanted to go to Lamaze classes even though I knew what I was doing, I would so he could experience it. He was already a great father. He helped me balance. I would cook, but not as much as we would eat fast food, so he pushed me to cook more, and he implemented a family structure. We sat down as a family, said grace, and ate every night.

I was praising God for blessing me to be able to give him a child, and we found out it was a boy. However, I dreamed that I was at my baby shower, with pink decorations and girl clothes given to me.

I discarded the dream and settled into the feelings of extreme happiness about the news of a boy. Three girls and two boys. We had already decided he would be a Jr. He gave me all my cravings, and everyone, including the kids, was so happy. This was finally a pregnancy with my husband and, not only that, *a man who loves me.*

On January 28, 2014, I was five months pregnant. We went to a regularly scheduled doctor's appointment. The nurse came in to do the usual, and as she listened for the heartbeat, she told me, "He wants to be stubborn today." She kept trying and trying, and her look changed.

She then said, "I'm going to get the doctor. She has a better ultrasound device." We didn't think anything once she said that. The doctor came in, and with her device in her hand, she tried to listen for his heartbeat.

I asked her if there was something wrong, and she said to me she didn't like what she saw but for me to follow her to the back to take another ultrasound. We went to the back, and she slid the handheld probe across my stomach. I started to worry, and when she was finished, she said to us, "I'm sorry to have to tell you this, but your baby is no longer alive."

I said, "There's no way!"

She responded, "I'm so sorry. I am sure of this. I will schedule you to be induced in a couple of days."

"Induced? I have to go through the full labor only not to hear his cry and go home with him?"

We both were devastated. We left, and my husband believed God for a miracle. I watched him speak over and pray over pregnant women, and it came to pass. When we got home, we still believed that God would give us a miracle. I remember telling my mom, and she was hurt. He told his mom, and she reminded him how it had happened to her. I was so upset and started asking why this was happening to me. I started blaming myself. All I could think of was that this was happening all because of me having that abortion. I hated myself.

Three days later, I had to check in at the hospital, and Jullian asked the doctor to check again. He still believed. This doctor was so nice and said, "Of course." She did right in front of us, shook her head, and said, "No, I'm so sorry."

He cried so hard, and there I was, going through not only labor pain but heartache and guilt.

After about eight hours or more, she told me when to push, and I did. He weighed around one pound. The doctor told me that he could remain in the room with us for as long as we wanted, and the nurse dressed him and took pictures. Because he was already gone before delivery, they didn't allow me to have a funeral nor name him, but we just called him J. Jr and the nurse told me all of the babies would be meeting at the gravesite on the same day. There were about ten of us there the day we were told to meet.

## CHAPTER 10
# *Our Heart's Desire*

We grieved for so long, but we still had to continue pastoring. I pushed myself to continue. We had a strong support system. Both of our mothers, the church family, Bishop Blackwell, and my two friends, Shanna and Shauniqua, were by my side. Even my biological mother was there for me, and she told me I would get pregnant again, but I didn't want to hear that. My friend Shauniqua told me that she went to God on my behalf because she didn't understand, and she told me that it's a part of my ministry and it's going to be to help others, but God would bless me again, and I definitely didn't want to hear that. I wanted my son. I didn't want to sing or preach. I was also told to allow Jullian a chance to grieve in his own way, and if he wanted to grieve alone, it was okay. He was being strong for me.

As time went by, I had good days and bad days. I decided to quit my job at the collection agency. I didn't even want to face them because everyone was happy. Many of them attended our wedding and knew Jullian was an answered prayer. My husband always ministered to me, but he *really* ministered and comforted me during this time. He told me that God would bless us again, that I wasn't being punished for the things I had done in my past, and that God had already forgiven me. He told me God knows the things we don't, and he chose to take him.

I prayed and asked God to forgive me for how angry I got and asked for him to help me through the hurt, pain, and disappointment and to allow me to genuinely be happy for other women who were getting pregnant all around me and going full term and delivering healthy babies. And God did just that. God also brought the dream back to my memory of when I was pregnant with our son at my baby shower, but it had pink decorations and girl clothes. And so I asked my husband, "What if God was showing me all along that I would have a girl?"

Six months later, I found out that I was pregnant again. I was considered high-risk because I had hypertension, and also I was almost 35, so they scheduled me with high-risk doctors, and I was fine with that. We decided not to publicize it at all. We told only immediate family and our trusted friends, and we told them *not* to publicize it.

It was in 2014 that we moved into our own church in Smithfield, VA and found favor there with a landlord. More people joined, and God continued to bless us. People would see my stomach, but I didn't confirm anything. I went to the doctor more often than usual, and they closely watched me.

I remember them asking me when I was around 12 weeks pregnant if I had experienced any bleeding because I had a vanishing twin. A vanishing twin is a type of miscarriage. It's when more than one embryo appears to be developing in the uterus and dies. It is then absorbed by the remaining fetus and mother[1].

I told them I hadn't dealt with any bleeding, and I asked if it would affect my baby, and they told me no. They continued monitoring me, and I found out that we were having a girl. Six months into the pregnancy, December

---

[1] What is Vanishing Twin Syndrome?
https://www.healthline.com/health/vanishing-twin

to be exact, they told me that I had decreased blood flow to the placenta and that I would have to stay in the hospital until the delivery. They told me they would keep her in there as long as they could. Although I knew my husband could hold down the house and the church, I did not want to be laying up in the hospital for months. But whatever it took to get her here and healthy, I didn't mind the sacrifice.

Each week, the doctors would write on the board the goal was to get through another week, and then they added that I was not to Google. I was in the hospital on Christmas and New Year's Day. They told me the plan was to induce her on February 14th. But on February 10, 2015, at 33 weeks, my blood pressure shot up so high they told me that they had to get her out and they had to prepare to prep me for a C-section.

I had all the other children naturally, so I became a bit nervous. Jullian had just left, and I called him and told him to turn around, "Babe, they are about to take her."

We had already signed the paperwork to tie my tubes, so I knew this was it. I didn't want to go through another high-risk pregnancy.

After they gave me the epidural, I just lay patiently, waiting for our baby blessing to be taken out. The doctor asked if we were sure we wanted to tie our tubes, and we both said "Yes."

It wasn't long at all, and the doctor told me that she was out, and my response was, "I want to hear her cry."

Jullian said, "She will," and I remember him trying to keep me as calm as possible.  He assured me she was well.

She weighed 3lbs 5oz. I was still on the table, and they gave her to my husband, and she just stared into his eyes. We had her for just a couple of minutes before they took her to the NICU, where she stayed for three weeks. My baby passed all of her tests, and we were able to take her home. I can't describe the feeling we both had. She was an answer to prayer, a miracle, and our heart's desire.

In 2015, not only did we have our baby, but we decided to move from Windsor, VA, where my mobile home was, and look for a place in Suffolk. My credit went down just a little bit once we married because we were one, so I took on some of his debt. I knew I could still fix his credit and that mine would go back to the 700's where it had been.

He always wanted to please me, and he did. I was good with the surprise chocolates and cards. He told me that when he came into his own and got on his feet, he would buy me the real Christian Louboutin Red Bottoms and a real Louis Vuitton handbag and put me in a house. I was just happy that I had a faithful and loving husband.

I decided to sell my mobile home and received good money for it. Remember, my parents helped me pay off my mobile home. My mother was okay with me selling it, but my siblings and some cousins always had something negative to say about me. I told my mom I would give her some money out of it for helping me purchase it and for all she had done for the wedding. We also needed to pay off some debt.

The mobile home sold quickly, and we moved to Suffolk, VA, where we rented both a house and a church. Our oldest daughter, by this time, had graduated from high school in 2016, and things were pretty good on the home side, but the church started to go through while in Suffolk, Va. That's where we experienced warfare on another level. We weren't growing as much there. A lot of people in that area went to the church their grandparents took them to when they were growing up.

We put on revivals and had many fundraisers. We kept plowing as much as we could. But we had people from Smithfield, and although that's where I was raised, it was a small town where everybody talked about everybody. So when people left our ministry, they joined in talking about us, but we never responded. That was easy for him but hard for me. I had a side I call the "pop off at any time and anywhere me." I prayed to keep that side of me under the blood.

After much prayer, my husband told me that Suffolk, VA, was not our region and the church would be in Newport News, VA, and I trusted his leading. One of many things I knew for sure was that he hears from God. So, we lived in Suffolk, and our church moved to  Newport News in 2016, where it currently resides to this day. The favor of God has always been on our lives, and we began to see the Lord move for us so many times.

Our second oldest graduated from High School in 2018, but also 2018 brought on grief. My husband's mother passed away on February 20, 2018, and that was a hard blow. I can honestly say I had the best Mother-N-Love anyone could ask for. She was the sweetest. She would come to stay with us from time to time, and I enjoyed every bit of it. I was so glad she got to spend time with us. She was saved and loved God, and my husband told me that's where he got his prophetic mantle from.

I remember on her deathbed when we went to visit her in the hospital. When we came into the room during one visit, Jullian said, "Hey, Mom, I'm here."

And she asked, "Where's Carolyn?"

"I'm here, Mom," I answered, and she grabbed my hand, and a presence filled the room. As she held my hand, she lifted herself up from lying down, and I could feel the power of God all over me. It felt as if something was going through my body. My husband told me later that it was an impartation, and then she laid back down. When she passed, I was just there for my husband and allowed him to grieve. I had never seen him so down so many days. But I just remained by his side. I was also happy that she saw him doing good for himself, and she left here knowing that he would be okay.

We had short-term goals, and there were long-term goals. As the years passed, we checked off the goals we accomplished. We always followed God. I trusted my husband's coverage and his guidance, and I handled the business. My husband has crazy faith, and even I went with it if he heard it, but sometimes I would say, "Babe, this will cost this."

He would ask, "Where's your faith?" And with hard work and discipline, we'd accomplish it.

We purchased our first home "together" on May 16, 2019. We both cried with excitement, but his excitement was on another level because he accomplished what he had never thought he could. *God* did this for us. We weren't perfect, but our hands were clean. We lived what we preached. If only his mom could have seen that day, but I told my mom, and she was happy. But there goes my family, who started a rumor saying that I didn't pay my mom back for what she did for me. Truth is, I could never pay my mom back for what she did for me. She had taken me and my biological brother in, adopted me, and taught me the ways of the Lord. You can't pay someone back for unconditional love, but we did honor our word and gave her some money. There was always chatter, but she knew what we had done and told me to love them anyway.

July 31, 2019, it felt like my whole world had crumbled. My mother, Nellie Mae King, went on to be with the Lord. I wouldn't wish that kind of pain on a worst enemy. Even though legally I was adopted and I had met my biological mother, Debra Pitt, and knew who she was. For me, my mom had just passed away. No more would I be able to see her or call her for advice and tell my problems to—no more grandma for the kids. I couldn't even properly grieve from still arguing with my family. I wasn't looking for one dime. I could honestly say I had more than money could buy; I had the favor of God in my life, and I was going to carry out her legacy. Everything that I watched her do as a wife and a mother with God first, I was going to continue to do. She was the epitome of strength.

At my mother's homegoing, I read the poem "A Mother's Crown" (author unknown). I had purchased several different gemstones and had each one of her grandchildren place one in the casket as I read.

Through it all, my husband was by my side, but I was still crushed. The woman who helped shape me and mold me into the woman I am today was gone. Although she got to see me grown, happily married, saved, and on fire for God, her absence was felt.

About a week later, I dreamed that I was walking on the street of her house, the house that I grew up in, and Jullian was with me, and all of a sudden, I saw something fall from the sky really fast. I walked closer until I got into the yard, which was on the side of the house near her window, to see what had fallen. It was a large, clear, beautiful crystal. As I looked closer at the crystal, the inside of it held each gemstone I'd purchased for the grandkids to place in her casket, which were a ruby, an emerald, a sapphire stone, a garnet stone, an amethyst, a pearl, and a diamond.

Jullian was going to touch it, and I told him not to touch it. In my subconscious, I was thinking it may have the same effect as if a star fell and thinking that it may be hot. I also remember the presence of a third person, but I never saw the face, but they were there. When I woke up, I told Jullian, and called my sis, the dream interpreter, and she confirmed what I knew to be true, and peace rushed over me.

I never asked about any insurance money or anything. I just held on to all the memories we shared and all the teachings she instilled in me. I was blessed, and if I continued to follow God, there was nothing that I wouldn't be able to obtain.

For the word says in Psalm 37:4 KJV, *"Delight thyself also in the LORD; and he shall give thee the desires of thine heart."* I also continued to stand on the word in Psalms 84:11 KJV: *"For the Lord God is a sun and shield: the Lord will give grace and glory: no good thing will he withhold from them that walk uprightly."*

I am who I am today because of my mother. God knew what and who I needed. God placed me in the right home. Everything that happened after adoption was already in God's plans. Jeremiah 29:11 KJV says, *For I know the thoughts that I think toward you, saith the LORD, thoughts of peace, and not of evil, to give you an expected end.* I salute my biological mother, Debra Pitt because she could have aborted me and termed my destiny and my purpose. Instead, she made the decision that she felt was best which was to put me up for adoption. She carried me for nine months and I'm thankful, and my mother took over when I was 18 months and carried me for almost 38 years and for that I'm grateful and blessed!

Looking over my life so far, all I can do is give God thanks because I love my life. I love being a mother to our five amazing children.

They bring me so much joy. They all have special, unique gifts, and each of them has their own relationship with God. I love being a wife to my amazing husband, Apostle Jullian Ricks, the man of my dreams and fulfillment of my prayers. He currently has his own shoe line and has written two songs that are streaming on all digital platforms. He now has excellent credit and multiple streams of income, and in 2022, he purchased a half-million-dollar church, "Church of Destiny," where I proudly work alongside him in ministry. He is also the founder and Presiding Prelate over Destiny International Fellowship, where he currently covers four churches. He is one of the most sought-after prophetic voices of this time.

And oh yeah, he did buy me those authentic Christian Louboutin red bottoms, over eight pairs to be exact, just like he said he would, and multiple Louis Vuitton authentic handbags. But most of all, he heard God when the Lord told him that I was his wife. God definitely ordained our marriage, and it feels like our love gets stronger every day. We celebrated our 10-year wedding anniversary in 2022 and renewed our vows. The same Bishop who counseled and married us in 2012 renewed our vows, which was amazing.

Last but not least, I love being a Pastor, where my husband is the senior Pastor to some amazing people. Church of Destiny is the best.

If you look at the "hand I was dealt" in life, I was in the foster care system as a baby, adopted, then a teenage mother – I should have been a statistic. BUT GOD! God had His hand on my life the entire time.

This is more than just my autobiography. I still have more life to live, this is just the beginning. This is the first part of my testimony and glimpse into my VICTORIOUS life after adoption.

(Pictured: Our vow renewal. Do you see the Red Bottoms?)

# About Carolyn Ricks

Pastor Carolyn V. Ricks is a sought-after empowerment preacher, revolutionary thinker, entrepreneur, and a powerhouse leader. She is considered a bold demon slayer, a woman of God who walks in total authority under the leading of the Holy Spirit.

As a catalyst for change and a voice of hope, she serves alongside her husband, Apostle Jullian T. Ricks, as the Pastor of Church of Destiny in Newport News, Virginia.

Pastor Carolyn Ricks was born on March 20, 1980, and matriculates from the Smithfield School system of Virginia. She is a compassionate and loving wife to Apostle Jullian T. Ricks and mother of five beautiful and radiant children. She is the CEO/Founder of Lady Carolyn Enterprise LLC (Custom Skirts and Apparel designed by Lady C).

Pastor Carolyn became a licensed minister under UHCOL, where Bishop William Blackwell Sr. serves as presiding prelate, in 2013. After years of faithful and committed service,

God released her and her husband to birth the Church of Destiny, where she was ordained Elder and currently affirmed as Pastor.

God has given Pastor Carolyn a passion for ministering to women who encounter life-altering challenges such as abuse, divorce, joblessness, grief, rejection, depression, and abandonment. When she preaches, she translates powerful spiritual truth into everyday language that empowers individuals to transform their lives and all of the lives connected to them. Pastor Carolyn is committed to hearing the voice of the Lord. She lays on her face and inclines her ear to only what He speaks. The prophetic mantle on her life has changed the lives of many. Miracles, signs, and wonders have come to pass. Women who once were told they had the inability to conceive have now bore children and are now a testament to the healing power of her hands through Christ Jesus. Her message brings forth purpose, meaning, and dignity.